KNOCK
KNOCK

KNOCK
KNOCK

A play by
Jules Feiffer

A MERMAID DRAMABOOK

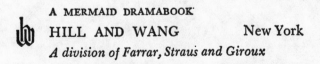

HILL AND WANG   New York
A division of Farrar, Straus and Giroux

To Sherlee Lantz

KNOCK KNOCK was first presented in New York City by the Circle Repertory Company (Jerry Arrow, Executive Director) on January 18, 1976. The play was directed by Marshall W. Mason, with the following cast:

COHN	DANIEL SELTZER
ABE	NEIL FLANAGAN
WISEMAN	JUDD HIRSCH
JOAN	NANCY SNYDER

Joan's Voices, the Bailiff's voice, and other apparitions were played by Judd Hirsch.

The setting was by John Lee Beatty, costumes by Jennifer von Mayrhauser, lighting by Dennis Parichy, and sound by Charles London and George Hansen. Dan Hild was the Production Stage Manager.

Later, producers Terry Allen Kramer and Harry Rigby moved the play to Broadway, where it opened at the Biltmore Theatre on February 24, 1976.

KNOCK
KNOCK

The time is the present. A small log house in the woods. It is un-painted, cramped, containing the worldy goods of two lifetimes, COHN's *and* ABE's. *Books and periodicals litter every surface, in-cluding the floor, which is covered with an old Persian rug. Two out-of-use TV's, circa 1950. An aged radio-phonograph console; next to it on the floor a stack of classical LP's. A large oak table that serves as a dining table and* ABE's *desk. A typewriter, hold-ing a blank sheet of paper at* ABE's *end of the table; next to it a ream of blank paper. The kitchen is separated from the living-dining room by a tattered screen, covered with magazine cut-outs of famous faces: Einstein, Tolstoy, Beethoven, Toscanini, F.D.R., Gandhi, Joe Louis, Babe Ruth, Katharine Cornell . . . The kitchen is well equipped: a huge iron range, shelves of spices, canned goods, other supplies. A shelf of cookbooks. Two burlap-curtained doorways lead to the bedrooms. A tiny win-dowed door leads outside. The view through two dark windows is of vegetation: crawling vines, blackened leaves. Pictures bury the walls: simply framed, very small, mostly family photographs and postcard-size reproductions of Impressionist paintings. Near the fireplace: a large steamer trunk. Somewhere close to the kitchen: an open ironing board; on it a graying bundle of shirts, living there for days. On a side table:* COHN's *violin; near it, a music stand. In addition to the two dining-room chairs there is an old rocker:* COHN's, *and a huge, beat-up, overstuffed armchair:* ABE's.

Act One

(AT RISE: COHN, *overweight and fifty, is at the stove, reading from a cookbook and mixing ingredients into a pot. He is humming a Mozart aria. He hums, cooks, tastes. Across the room,* ABE, *underweight and fifty, lies in his chair staring into space. He lights a cigar and meditates.*)

ABE

It's getting better.

COHN

(*Tastes.*)

Who says?

ABE

I say.

COHN

(*Mixes.*)

With what evidence?

ABE

My eyes are my evidence.

COHN
(*Turns to* ABE *and raises two fingers.*)
How many fingers?

ABE
Five.

COHN
Some eyes.
(*Goes back to his cooking.*)

ABE
All right, two.

COHN
(*Slams down the pot and turns to* ABE.)
So if you can see two, why do you say five?

ABE
I prefer five.

COHN
That's not a reason.

ABE
Why does there always have to be a reason?

COHN
Abe, I've known you for twenty-five years and for you there's never a reason.

ABE
And you? You're better off?

COHN
I don't invent.

ABE
I beg your pardon. Neither do I.

COHN
What kind of fool am I living with? You just made up five.

ABE

I didn't make it up.

COHN

Not a minute ago.

ABE

No.

COHN

I was holding up two (*Holds up two fingers.*) and you said I was
holding up five! (*Holds up five fingers.*)

ABE

You *are* holding up five.
(COHN *quickly puts down his hand.*)

COHN

What's the use?

ABE

Cohn, I'll tell you something—you're rigid. I'm flexible.

COHN

Mindless.

ABE

You only believe in what's in front of your nose. That's not
mindless?

COHN

I don't make things up.

ABE

(*Points to curtained doorway.*)
What's that?

COHN

Don't bother me. (ABE *continues to point.*) It's my bedroom!
(*Goes back to his cooking.*) Pest!

ABE

I don't see any bedroom.

COHN

You know it's my bedroom!

ABE

I beg your pardon. All I see is a curtain. (COHN *goes and pulls back the curtain.*) Ah hah! A bedroom! (ABE *rises, crosses to the doorway, and pulls the curtain back into place.*) A curtain. (*Pulls the curtain back and forth.*) A bedroom. A curtain. A bedroom. A curtain. A bedroom. Is it still a bedroom when you don't see it?

COHN

It's always a bedroom!

ABE

So for you it's always a bedroom and for me it's always five fingers. (COHN *slams the plate down on the table, pours stew into it, and begins to eat.* ABE *joins him at the table, studies the blank sheet in his typewriter, punches one key, and nods seriously at the results.*) I'm right, so I don't get any stew?

COHN

You want stew? Here!
(*Hands him pot.*)

ABE

(*Looks into pot.*)
It's empty.

COHN

(*Points to empty pot.*)
What's that?

ABE

A pot.

COHN

You saw me cook stew in it? (ABE *nods.*) You saw me pour stew out of it? (ABE *nods.*) So eat your stew. (ABE, *unhappily, watches* COHN *eat.* COHN *wipes his mouth and points to the*

empty space in front of ABE.) Eat! That's steak. That's potatoes.
That's salad. That's beer. Hearty appetite!

ABE
That's vicious.

COHN
(*Smiles, self-satisfied.*)
Abe, you can pull the wool over your eyes but you can't pull it
over mine. I know you every step of the way. I know you inside
and out.

ABE
I'm hungry.

COHN
So make something.

ABE
You know I don't cook. I burn everything.

COHN
Don't.

ABE
My mind wanders. (COHN *gets up, crosses to stock shelf; takes
down a box of spaghetti, sets a plate in front of* ABE, *and pours
the uncooked spaghetti into the plate.*) It's not cooked.

COHN
I say it's cooked. Two fingers. Five fingers. Eat your spaghetti.
(ABE *looks disconsolately at the plate, picks the spaghetti sticks
up in his hand, and begins to eat them.* COHN *watches for a moment then relents. He takes the plate away from* ABE *and pours
the spaghetti into a pot of water on the stove.*) When will you
learn?

ABE
To be like you? I beg your pardon, is that such a blessing?

COHN

Don't get personal.

ABE

I don't like being made a fool of.

COHN

You asked for it.

ABE

I know I'm right. (COHN *groans*.) You can win the argument but it doesn't mean you're right. Inside I know who's right.

COHN

You think so?

ABE

I know so. With my ex-wife, I also lost all arguments. But you told me I was right.

COHN

With her you *were* right.

ABE

So if I lost with her and was right, you have to admit that when I lose with you I also could be right. It's consistent.

COHN

Abe, I'm going to tell you a little story. A parable. After I finish, you tell me what it means to you. O.K.?

ABE

Before I eat?

COHN

Here. (*Cuts him a slice of cheese.* ABE *wolfs it down.*) Once there was this beautiful, innocent, young maid, golden locks, of eighteen, who lived in a dark forest in the country with her very proud, strict parents, and it was her habit to sit by a pond day in and day out, and moon and mope about the moment when love would first enter her life. One day this lovely young thing is daydreaming by the pond when a frog hops out of the water and into her lap. The beautiful maid recoils. "Don't be frightened," croaks the ugly little frog, "I am not what I appear to be. I am in truth a handsome young prince cast under a spell by a wicked witch and this spell can only be broken when some fair maid takes me into her bed and spends the night by my side." So the girl calms down and decides why not? So she brought the frog home and she took it to bed with her and the next morning she woke up—and lying next to her was this tall, handsome, naked young prince. And that's the way she explained it to her parents when they walked in on the two of them. What's the moral of the story?

ABE

The moral is, you're a very cynical man.

COHN

You want dinner? Then discuss it intelligently.

ABE

(*Leaves the table and returns to his own chair.*)
The moral is, you take a classic fable with charm and beauty, that deals with dreams and imagination, and you change it into men's-room humor. That's the moral. What you reveal of yourself.
(*Leaves his chair, crosses to the typewriter, punches a key, and sits back down again.*)

COHN

You would believe the girl's story?

ABE

I beg your pardon, I wouldn't be her prosecutor. I leave that to you.

COHN

Supposing you're the girl's father?

ABE

I would face the problem with compassion.

COHN

First admitting it's a problem!

ABE

A man in bed with my daughter? At first—until the situation's cleared up, I have to admit it's a problem.

COHN

Then she tells you the story of the frog.

ABE

Which clears up everything.

COHN

You believe about the frog?

ABE

What's important is, she believes about the frog. We didn't bring her up to lie.

COHN

You'd rather have her crazy than lie.

ABE

Why is that crazy?

COHN

Or hallucinating.

ABE

Because her mind can conjure with change—with ugliness turning into beauty—you call that hallucinating? And what *you* see —only beauty turning into ugliness—you call that reality? I beg your pardon, Cohn, you're living in a stacked deck. You give me a choice, I prefer frogs into princes over princes into frogs.

COHN

Even if it's not so.

ABE

How do we know? All I'm saying is, we don't know.

COHN

Do we know that you're Abe and I'm Cohn.

ABE

In this life.

COHN

In this life. But in another life, maybe I was Abe and you were Cohn?

ABE

It's possible. Anything's possible.

COHN

—or that I was Mozart and you were Thomas Jefferson?

ABE

It's unlikely. But it's possible.

COHN

—or that I was Moses and you were Christ?

ABE

It's possible.

COHN

Abe, I'm going to give you a chance to listen to what you just said: It's possible you were Christ.

ABE

I didn't say probable. I said possible.

COHN

And it's possible that if I rub this lamp a genie will come out?

ABE

All I'm saying is, we don't know, do we?

(COHN *rubs the lamp.*)

COHN

Now we know.

ABE

I beg your pardon, we know about one lamp. We don't know about all lamps. Also, we don't know that a genie *didn't* come out. We don't know that there isn't a genie in this room this very moment. And that he isn't saying, "Master, I am the genie of the lamp and I have three wishes to grant you and anything you wish will come true." Maybe he's there and maybe we've been taught how not to see genies in our time. Or hear them. Or take advantage when they offer us three wishes. That's all I'm saying. That it could be us, not him.

COHN

Who?

ABE

The genie.

COHN

Abe, if I had three wishes, you know what would be my first wish? That instead of you to talk to, to drive me crazy for another twenty years, I had somebody with a brain I could talk to! That's what I wish!

(*A sudden explosion engulfs* ABE. *Light and music effect. The smoke clears, and sitting in his place is a bearded* WISE MAN *in robes. He holds a clipboard and a pen.*)

WISEMAN

Name?!

COHN

(*Shaken*)

Cohn.

WISEMAN

(*Checks the clipboard.*)

That's right—Cohn. Occupation?!

COHN

Musician.

WISEMAN

(*Smiles.*)

Musician. Where are you a musician, Cohn?

COHN

At the present I am unemployed.

WISEMAN

(*Smiles.*)

At the present you are unemployed, is that right, Cohn?

COHN

Yes.

WISEMAN

At the present—let me see if I have this straight—you are an unemployed musician.

COHN

That's right.

WISEMAN

Unemployed. But still a musician.

COHN

Yes.

WISEMAN

What are you first, Cohn? A musician or an unemployed?

COHN

I don't understand the question.

WISEMAN

You wanted someone intelligent to talk to?

COHN

Yes.

WISEMAN

Meaning that he will be on your level. That's what you mean by intelligent, isn't it Cohn? (*Waits.*) Well? Isn't it?

COHN

I guess it is.

WISEMAN

By that we are to assume that you consider yourself intelligent. Or do I go too far, Cohn?

COHN

No.

WISEMAN

No what?

COHN

What you said.

WISEMAN

That I go too far?

COHN

(*Inaudible*)
No.

WISEMAN

I can't hear you.

COHN

The other—what else you said first.

WISEMAN

That you consider yourself—don't let me put words in your mouth—intelligent. Though unemployed, out of work, a ward of the state, you consider yourself intelligent. And that you want as a companion—am I right in this?—someone of equal intelligence. I am not putting words in your mouth?

COHN

No. Equal intelligence. That's it.

WISEMAN
You want another unemployed musician?

COHN
Look—what's happened to Abe?

WISEMAN
Who?

COHN
Abe—my friend.

WISEMAN
You want Abe?

COHN
I want to know where he went.

WISEMAN
You miss this Abe? Is he another unemployed musician?

COHN
A stockbroker. Mutual funds. Retired.

WISEMAN
A wealthy retired stockbroker.

COHN
Yes.

WISEMAN
Supporting you?

COHN
He was sitting in that chair.

WISEMAN
In my chair?

COHN
It's Abe's chair.

WISEMAN
It's Wiseman's chair.

COHN
Who?

WISEMAN
Myself. Helmut Wiseman. It is my chair. You see? I am sitting in it. See how I sit in it, relax in it, lean back in it? So whose chair would you say this is? Does it look as if I've ever been out of this chair? Conversely, does it not look as if I have always been in this chair? How tall is this Abe?

COHN
Five foot eight.

WISEMAN
He is too short for this chair. You either have the wrong man or the wrong chair. Or the wrong height. If you had another height you might have the right man. But it would still be the wrong chair. No, I'm sorry, I can't help you. This is my chair. I, Wiseman. Mine. I know—you must have the wrong house! Try next door.

COHN
This is my house.

WISEMAN
(*He refers to his clipboard.*)
Whose?

COHN
(*Quickly*)
Abe's. Abe and I live here.

WISEMAN
In this house?

COHN
Yes!

WISEMAN

Or a house very much like this?

COHN

It's *this* house!

WISEMAN

It can't be this house because it's not the right chair.

COHN

It *is* the right chair!

WISEMAN

Then why isn't Abe sitting here? You see, Cohn, your argument collapses of its own weight. I'm sorry, I would like to spend more time with you, but there are others waiting. Will you send in the next applicant, please

COHN

What?

WISEMAN

(*Points to door.*)

On your way out, will you send in the next applicant? (*A knock on the door.*) You see, they are getting impatient.

COHN

This is *my* house!

WISEMAN

Your house? Well, I like that! Now you see here, Mr. Wiseman—

COHN

You're *Wiseman*!

WISEMAN

(*Indignant*)

Oh! And I suppose I'm Cohn!

COHN

I'm Cohn!

WISEMAN

Now *you're* Cohn. It's your chair, your house, and your Cohn. Then who am I, may I ask?

COHN

I don't know who you are! You barge in here—

WISEMAN

Barge in? Did you see me barge in?

COHN

In a manner of speaking.

WISEMAN

No, I'm sorry, Mr. Wiseman, or whatever you call yourself, I don't at all care for your manner of speaking. Your manner of speaking is offensive to me. Now if you had a nicer manner of speaking, something like: (*Sweet-voiced*) "Hello. How are you? I like you. Will you be my friend?" Well, that would be another manner entirely. But the way things stand now, the position is already filled. (*Knock on door.*) And tell the others to come back tomorrow. I'm going to bed. (WISEMAN *rises and disappears behind the curtained doorway leading into* COHN's *bedroom.*) —A terrible day. I want to leave a call for seven. (COHN *crosses to the doorway.*) If you don't have seven in stock, make it nine.

(*Another knock.* COHN *turns to the door.*)

COHN

Who—who's there?

JOAN

Joan.

COHN

Joan who?

JOAN
(*Sings.*)
Joan know why there's no sun up in the sky, stormy weather.

(COHN *growls and grabs the poker from the fireplace.*)

COHN
Enough's enough! (*To* JOAN) Did you hear? Enough is enough!

WISEMAN
Will you kids quiet it down in there!

COHN
(*Whirls toward bedroom.*)
Wiseman!! (*Advances on bedroom with poker.*) I warn you
I'm armed!! (*He disappears behind the curtain. Sounds of a
fight. Curtain moves violently. After a moment* WISEMAN *skips
out, opens the refrigerator, takes out a carrot, and skips back.
Throughout* WISEMAN'*s exit and return the sound of the fight
and the bustling of the curtain continue. A moment later,* COHN
*crawls out of the bedroom, his clothes in tatters. He throws open
the trunk in the corner and pulls out a shotgun. He crawls back
inside the bedroom with the shotgun. A loud blast.* COHN *staggers out, dragging the dead* WISEMAN. *Knock on the door.* COHN
freezes, holding WISEMAN.) Who's there?

JOAN
Joan.

COHN
Joan who?

JOAN
Joan ask me no questions and I'll tell you no lies.

(COHN *drags* WISEMAN *over to the trunk and with great
difficulty manages to squeeze him into it. But not all of him. He
pushes down on the head and the legs pop out. He sticks the legs*

back in and the head and shoulders slide up. This goes on for a
while until finally all of WISEMAN *is in the trunk and* COHN *slams*
shut the lid, at which point the side collapses and WISEMAN'S *legs*
pop out. COHN *stares sullenly at* WISEMAN'S *exposed legs. An-*
other knock.)

COHN
(Wearily)
Joan who?

JOAN
(Sings.)
Joan sit under the apple tree with anyone else but me.

COHN
I thought so.
(He folds back the edge of the rug, slides the trunk next to it,
then unfolds the rug over WISEMAN'S *legs. He skulks back into*
the bedroom and comes out with the shotgun. He crosses to the
door and listens. During the above we hear the following outside
the door.)

JOAN
He won't let me in.

FIRST VOICE
He has to!

SECOND VOICE
Did you tell him who you are?

JOAN
No.

FIRST VOICE
Tell him.

JOAN
I can't.

SECOND VOICE
Why not?

JOAN
It sounds like name-dropping.

FIRST VOICE
Maybe he hasn't heard of you.

JOAN
He must have heard of me.

SECOND VOICE
How do you know if you don't tell him.

(*Pause.*)

JOAN
Knock. Knock.

COHN
(*Reloads shotgun.*)
Who's there?

JOAN
Joan.

COHN
(*Getting ready.*)
Joan who?

JOAN
Joan of Arc. (COHN *whips open the door and blasts away. A loud clang.* COHN *recoils in horror, drops the gun, and backs off. In walks a vision of loveliness wearing a suit of armor. The breastplate has a big black dent in it.* JOAN *glares at* COHN, *crosses herself, and starts talking to her body.*) Are you all right?

FIRST VOICE
I'm all right—a little shaky.

SECOND VOICE
I'm upset but I'm all right.

COHN
(*Gasping.*)
Who are you?

FIRST VOICE
That's some greeting.

SECOND VOICE
You got any more surprises like that?

COHN
Who are they?

JOAN
(*Taps the dent in her armor.*)
My Voices.

(COHN *retreats to the curtained doorway, turns quickly, and throws the shotgun into the bedroom, then turns back to* JOAN.)

COHN
I'm not a violent man—

(*A loud blast from the bedroom.* COHN *ducks his head behind the curtain and out again.*)

FIRST VOICE
He's a pacifist.

SECOND VOICE.
I'd like to pacifist *him* right in the mouth.

COHN
No harm done. Has this been a day! Look— (*Slowly regaining confidence through the sound of his own voice.*) Certain things we know. I'll make myself clear. We know that maturity is the

weaning out of synthetics in one's life, so that where in one's childhood, one's life was a will-o'-the-wisp, fantasy-laden, hodge-podge, over the years it develops into a spare, clear-eyed, precise, concise, essentially organic whole. Ask questions. I'm not a pedant.

JOAN
You think life is a hole. Life is holy, not a hole.

COHN
An organic whole.
(*Indicates with motion of his hand.*)

JOAN
Small wonder you go around shooting people. You don't know what's important.

COHN
I don't shoot people.

FIRST VOICE
You want to know where the hole is?

SECOND VOICE
In your head!

COHN
Look—(*A long exasperated pause.*) Who are they?

JOAN
My Voices? (COHN *nods.*) They're my Voices.

COHN
(*Restraining himself.*)
What have you got inside there? A tape recorder?

JOAN
(*Crosses herself.*)
You pitiful man. (*Places a hand on his shoulder.*) We must be on our way. Are these rags all you own?

COHN
I don't leave here.

JOAN
But you must come with me—

COHN
No!

JOAN
To see the Emperor!

COHN
Emperor—(*Quickly back-pedals, and bangs into the trunk.* WISEMAN's *legs kick up in the air under the rug.*) I'll make a contribution— (*Reaches into his pocket.*)

JOAN
I want you!

COHN
I live here. I stay here. Take the trunk! It's a gift!

JOAN
My mission is to bring you, among others, before the Emperor. It is your duty to follow me.

COHN
(*Retreats behind curtain.*)
You're barking up the wrong tree. I never leave here. Ask anyone. They never see me leave here. They don't know me. Ask anyone if they know me. They'll say, "Who?"

JOAN
You must do as I say!

COHN
I have to go with you to see the Emperor. What Emperor? What for? To tell him the sky is falling?

JOAN
The sky is not falling.

COHN
(*Sarcastic*)
Thank God!

JOAN
It is missing.

COHN
(*Comes out from behind curtain with change of clothes.*)
What's missing?

JOAN
The sky is missing! We must find the Emperor to give him the wonderful news that the sky is missing and that mankind's path to heaven is at last unblocked and unimpeded, and that God calls on His Highness, the Emperor, to build a thousand spaceships and put on them two of every kind and blast off for heaven. Before the holocaust.

COHN
(*Sits her down.*)
O.K. (*Pause.*) Let's take this a little bit at a time. First of all, there's an emperor, right? (JOAN *nods.*) And he lives—where *does* he live? (JOAN *points.*) He lives that way. (JOAN *nods.*) And you are heading a delegation of citizens to petition the Emperor to build a spaceship—

JOAN
A thousand spaceships!

COHN
To take us to, you said heaven, am I right? (JOAN *nods.*) Because the sky which has always been up there is not up there any more. (JOAN *nods.*) In fact, it is missing. And we are to bring this piece of news to the Emperor, this man you call the Emperor. And he is to put two of every kind on spaceships—and thus save us from the holocaust. JOAN *nods.*) And everybody else dies. We're saved. Everybody else dies. Is that a mission or is that a mission!

JOAN

Don't be dense; it has nothing to do with dying. It's more or less like moving. Some people live in the city and some people live in the suburbs and some people live in the country and some people live in heaven.

COHN

You don't have to die to go to heaven any more?

JOAN

Not since the sky is missing. You simply *move* there. But first, of course, you have to know it's there. For example, if your entire life were spent in the city, would you know about cows and trees? No! Well, it's no different with heaven. True, we may know about it in a *religious* sense, but certainly not as a place to migrate.

COHN

(*With infinite patience*)

But isn't it cruel—maybe cruel is too strong a word—isn't it thoughtless to abandon everyone else to the holocaust?

JOAN

(*Brightly*)

I'm glad you asked me that question. I, too, thought it was cruel, but my Voices tell me that people will never know it's a holocaust. They'll adapt themselves. Many may even find happiness. (*Goes to door.*) Are you ready?

COHN

Young lady, sit down, I have some shocking news to break to you. (*He sits* JOAN *back down in a chair.*) There is no Emperor.

JOAN

You might as well say there is no God.

COHN

There is no God.

JOAN

You might as well say there is no me and there is no you.

COHN

There is a me; that's all I concede.

JOAN

But there is no me?

COHN

For your information, you are not Joan of Arc.

JOAN

And my Voices?

COHN

There are no Voices.

FIRST VOICE

There are too!

COHN

There are not!

SECOND VOICE

Are too! Are too!

COHN

Are not! Are not!

FIRST AND SECOND VOICES

Are! Are! Are!

COHN

Not! Not! Not!

JOAN

Then whom are you arguing with?

COHN

(*Calms down.*)
It's not an argument, just a discussion. I wish you'd tell me how you do that.

JOAN

Have you never believed in anything?

COHN

I believe in me. After that there's room for doubt.

JOAN

But it's so lonely!

COHN

That's my problem.

JOAN

How can you bear it?

COHN

If you're strong, you can bear what's true. If you're weak, you make up fairy tales.

JOAN

You think I make up fairy tales?

COHN

I'm not signaling you out. Abe, my best friend. Him also. *He'd* go with you to see the Emperor. Not that he'd believe. He wouldn't believe. But just in case. With Abe it's always just in case. He's built an ethic out of "maybe," "who's to know," "just in case." (*In a rage*) He has no convictions! *No convictions!* I much prefer someone crazy like you who thinks she's Joan of Arc. That at least is a position. So that's another reason. I have to stay in the house to take care of Abe; I can't go with you to see the Emperor.

JOAN

We'll take him with us!

COHN

He's not here.

JOAN

Where is he?

COHN

That's the question. Vanished! Vanished to annoy me. You watch. I'll pay him back good. We had an argument—I won't bore you with the details—but it got around—who knows how? —to wishes. Two grown men, an argument over wishes. Abe said it's possible I had three, I said baloney. Abe said I couldn't know unless I wished, so I wished Abe would stop bothering me and vanish, and to make a long story short, in order to aggravate me, he did.

JOAN
Wish him back.

COHN
If life were only so simple.

JOAN
The first wish worked.

COHN
A trick.

JOAN
Are you afraid?

COHN
(Smiles.)
Afraid? Of what? Of wishes? Of voices? The only thing I'm afraid of is insanity. And that's a losing battle.

JOAN
I believe in your wishes!

COHN
That's reassuring.

JOAN
I do!

COHN
(Shakes his head sadly.)
What do you know? Nothing. No background. I'll make a bet, no education. What do you have for credentials? Nothing!

FIRST AND SECOND VOICES
Us!

COHN

Less than nothing!

JOAN

I was once very much like you.

COHN

(*Enraged*)

No one was ever like me! (*Calms himself.*) Don't be presumptuous.

JOAN

I was sad all the time.

COHN

I'm not sad.

JOAN

In despair.

COHN

This isn't despair.

JOAN

What do you call it?

COHN

Realism.

JOAN

Then why is it so much like despair?

COHN

I didn't say they're not connected. But they're not the same. With despair you feel there's no hope so you might as well die; with realism you feel there's no hope but you get a kick out of it.

JOAN

I wanted to die!

COHN

See? We're oceans part.

JOAN

I lived in a sea of despair—

COHN

Not the same!

JOAN

—with my wicked stepmother and her two wicked daughters.

COHN

Wait. You're confused. That's Cinderella.

JOAN

Exactly.

COHN

You're Joan of Arc.

JOAN

Oh, I don't mean *now*.

COHN

You used to be Cinderella?

JOAN

Of course!

COHN

But now you're Joan of Arc? (JOAN *nods, patiently.*) Well, you're certainly working your way up in the world. Of course, instead of marrying Prince Charming, you get burned at the stake, but you do make sainthood, while all Cinderella gets is to live happily ever after. And in one case Shaw writes about you and in the other case Walt Disney. All in all, I'd say you made a wise choice.

JOAN

Choice? What choice? After the ball, I thought the Prince loved me and I dreamed—well, no matter what I dreamed—he came looking for me, door to door, with a glass slipper. Like a salesman! . . . Can you imagine my shame? That he, my true love, would only know me by trying a shoe on my foot! I walked barefoot on rocks, soaked my feet in brine, anything to fail such a test. But it was never to be made. One door away from ours the Prince was suddenly called to war and I was left with a broken heart and a size-nine foot. So I became a nun. A very poor nun. Night after night, visions of Our Lord came to me bearing a glass slipper. So I fled the nunnery and traveled the land as a migrant fruit picker. I married and begat five Portuguese children. My husband was a sot and beat me. When my children grew of age, they beat me. So I threw myself off a bridge into the river. I landed on my feet and, to my considerable surprise, saw that I was standing on the water. I walked on the water for miles trying to decipher the meaning of my fate. Half mad with the complexities of it all, I tried again to drown myself, this time by standing on my head and ducking it under the water. But the farther under I ducked, the more the water level receded, until finally, the river ran dry. I knew that it was a sign! I fell to my knees and prayed God for His forgiveness and that I should prove myself worthy of being His servant. And on the fortieth day my Voices came and told me who I was and what I must do. And now, praise God, I am Joan and I am here!

COHN
(*Stares at her. After a long silence.*)
I really miss Abe.

JOAN
You don't believe my story.

COHN
You can walk on water, bring back Abe.

JOAN
Voices? May I?

FIRST VOICE
He shoots us and then he wants favors.

SECOND VOICE
He's got two more wishes. Why come to us?

COHN
Oy.

JOAN
You can.

COHN
I can't.

JOAN
Try.

COHN
I tried once. Look what happened!

JOAN
It came true.

COHN
It didn't come true. Certain things happened—I can't go into details—you don't know everything—

JOAN
You refuse to wish.

COHN
Let's drop the subject.

JOAN
You don't want it to come true.

COHN
I said—

JOAN
You don't want your friend back.

COHN
I want quiet! I want peace and quiet!

JOAN
But not your friend.

COHN
Him too! But first, quiet!

JOAN
Then wish!

COHN
You're a child!

JOAN
Wish!

COHN
Games!

JOAN
Wish!

COHN
Nag! Shrew! I wish! All right? I wish!

JOAN
What?

COHN
I wish Abe was back! (*Light and music effect.*) You satisfied? So where is he? You see him? Where is he? (JOAN *looks around.*) You're so smart. (*She looks in the bedroom.*) Miss Know-it-all.
(*He turns his back on her in contempt. She comes out of the bedroom, opens the lid of the trunk, and looks in.*)

JOAN
It came true!

(COHN *whirls, looks on in horror*)

COHN
Close it! What are you doing in there? Mind your own business!

JOAN
Come! Look!

COHN
Who do you think you are!

JOAN
Dear God! He's dead! (*Crosses herself.* COHN *retreats.*)
Your friend is dead.

COHN
He's not dead.

JOAN
He is dead.

COHN
He's dead. But Abe's not dead.

JOAN
But this is Abe.

COHN
He's not Abe. Abe is alive.

JOAN
You poor man. Your mind has cracked in grief. This is Abe.

COHN
Abe is shorter.

JOAN
This man is short.

COHN
Abe doesn't have a beard.

JOAN
The man is clean-shaven.

COHN
Abe is gray.

JOAN
In life this man was gray.

COHN
(*Crosses over to the trunk, fed up.*) For once and for all—
(*Looks in trunk.*) Abe! (*Falls into the trunk in a dead faint,
headfirst.* JOAN *rushes to trunk, pulls* COHN *out by his shoulders,
and tries to lift him off his knees.*) Go away. Leave me alone.
(*He rises shakily, staggers on the run behind his curtained doorway. After the briefest of pauses,* JOAN *follows.*)

JOAN
I know what's on your mind.

COHN
Go. The Emperor's waiting. *Give it back!*

(COHN's *shotgun comes flying out through the curtain, lands on
floor beyond trunk.*)

JOAN
What if *I* brought him back to life?

COHN
Lady—

JOAN
Would you then go with me to see the Emperor?

COHN
Oy!

JOAN
If I brought Abe back to life?

COHN
If you brought Abe back to life, I'd believe you were Jesus Christ
himself. Don't hit me!

JOAN
Don't blaspheme!

COHN
Don't nag!

JOAN
Would you believe?

COHN
Would I believe? I'd believe! I'd believe!

(ABE's *legs twitch.*)

JOAN
That I am Joan?

COHN
All right!

JOAN
And you will follow me?

COHN
All right!

JOAN
Praise the Lord!

(ABE's *twitch again. His head appears out of the trunk. He climbs out, looks at his typewriter, punches a key, and crosses to the refrigerator.*)

ABE
Cohn! What's to eat? (COHN *appears in the doorway. He cannot believe his eyes. He starts to collapse.* JOAN *catches him and helps him to a chair.* ABE *turns around and sees them. He shuts the refrigerator door and stares coldly at* JOAN.) Company?

COHN
You're dead.

ABE
(*Coldly*)
I didn't know you were having a party.

COHN
You're walking—you're talking—
(*He rises, starts to* ABE.)

ABE
I hope I'm not getting in the way. I know nobody invited me. I
just live here.

COHN
(*Goes to* ABE *and embraces him.*) He lives, he breathes—
(*Holds* ABE *away from him and stares at him happily.*) He
smells!

ABE
You're drunk.

COHN
(*To* JOAN)
Has there ever been such a friend, to rise from the dead in a rot-
ten mood? I love this man! (*Hugs* ABE. ABE *breaks free.*)

ABE
I beg your pardon. That person?

COHN
That's Joan! Joan, here's Abe!

ABE
I beg your pardon. An old friend?

COHN
How old is old? Ten minutes? A half hour? It feels like half a
lifetime. It was *your* lifetime, that I'll tell you!

ABE

Riddles. You invited her?

COHN

Not two minutes ago you were dead.

ABE

You wish.

COHN

I wished you back. They sent you back dead.

ABE

Intrigue is going on here. This is my house. I beg your pardon, miss. It's not personal. The house is in my name. But can I ever invite guests? Who was my last guest? Fifteen years ago. I'll show you the guest book. Look—here's the guest book. Blank, see? Hundreds of pages—wait, here's the guest—no, it reminds me— not even a real guest—a Jehovah's Witness. Came in out of the blue. We had coffee, a pleasant chat about religion. Cohn, here, throws a fit. Facts are facts, Cohn. It's nothing personal, miss. Cohn and I don't entertain. He agreed and I agreed. When we entertain we differ. It ends up in a fight. So we agreed to live and let live and not entertain. I didn't make up the rule. Now he breaks it. Is this a way to run a household? Anarchy?! I beg your pardon, Cohn, I thought we'd agreed—anarchy is for outside.

COHN
(*To* JOAN)
Is that a mouth? I love that mouth! (*Beaming at him.*) Abe, not five minutes ago you know what you were?

ABE

What?

COHN

You weren't! That's what you were. You were *not!* You were dead! You were dead! You were dead! (*Smile slowly fades.*) You weren't dead. (*Turns to* JOAN.) He wasn't dead.

JOAN
He was dead.

COHN
How could he be alive if he was dead?

JOAN
You saw him!

COHN
For half a second.

JOAN
He was cold.

COHN
Who felt him?

JOAN
I did!

COHN
I thought you were a saint. Now you're a doctor?

JOAN
You're reneging on your promise.

COHN
Don't be foolish; he only fainted.

ABE
I didn't faint.

COHN
You fainted.

ABE
Never!

COHN
In the trunk.

ABE

In what trunk?

COHN

That trunk!

ABE

I never fainted in a trunk in my life.

COHN

Not five minutes ago!

ABE

Five minutes ago I was sitting in my chair like always.

COHN

Then how come you didn't see her come in? (ABE *is stopped*.) Because you fainted!

ABE

Because you sneaked her in here before! When I wasn't looking!

COHN

What before?

ABE

Who knows, with a man as corrupt as you?! It could have been *years!* Who is she? Why is she wearing that armor?!

COHN

You're all excited. Calm down.

ABE

I don't like betrayal. I beg your pardon.

COHN

There's no betrayal.

ABE

Consorting with the outside.

COHN

No—

ABE

Spreading false rumors.

COHN

Abe, listen—calm now—what's the very last thing you remember?

ABE

Your betrayal.

COHN

(*Reasonably*)
Abe, *I* fainted and *I* remember.

ABE

I never fainted in my life! I beg your pardon, but I have never vomited, I have never fainted, and I have never gotten drunk. Certain things I do not do. I have never done. So you and your chippie, don't try to pull a fast one.

COHN

(*Stares hard at him.*)
You were dead. (*To* JOAN) It's the only explanation. He was dead.

ABE

I didn't faint so I must be dead. That's logic.

COHN

Not now, before.

ABE

How could I be dead before and alive now? That's consistency.

COHN

Wait a minute! Stop the presses! Is this my old friend Abe talking? The very Abe who believes in genies and three wishes and that I could be Mozart and him Jefferson?

ABE

There's no inconsistency.

COHN
No inconsistency?!

ABE
It's perfectly plausible that I could die Abe and come back some-
body else, but is it plausible that I should die Abe and come back
Abe?

COHN
Is it plausible that you should die *Jefferson* and come back Abe?

ABE
—in the same house, with the same Cohn? A frog into a prince I
could believe. Change! That's plausible! But sameness! Eternal
sameness! No, I beg your pardon, I can't be convinced.

COHN
(*Exasperated*)
I'm through wasting my breath.

(JOAN *crosses to* ABE. *He backs away. She takes his hand and
stares into his eyes.*)

JOAN
I am Joan of Arc.

ABE
It's possible. You could be anybody. I won't fight over it.

COHN
He doesn't believe you.

ABE
It doesn't matter what I believe, it's what you believe.

COHN
She believes you were dead!

ABE
(*To* COHN)
That's her privilege.

JOAN

You *were* dead.

ABE

(*To* JOAN)

As far as you were concerned. You never saw me, I never saw you. In that sense I was dead.

JOAN

I brought you back to life.

ABE

In a physical way? Well, who knows? It's been a long time. But I do feel a certain arousal—

COHN

(*Groans and buries his head in his hands.*)

It's not opinion! It's not an argument. It's a fact. A fact! A fact! She's Joan of Arc! She has Voices! She brought you back to life! (*To* JOAN) Strike him dead and bring him back again! (*To* ABE) And this time pay attention!

ABE

You ask me, is this Abe? I ask you, is this Cohn? You believe she's Joan of Arc?

COHN

No doubt about it.

ABE

And I was dead?

COHN

No question.

ABE

And she brought me back to life?

COHN

Believe me, it's a mixed blessing.

ABE
(*To* JOAN)
Huh—must you be able to argue!

COHN
I believe in what's concrete—in what I see, until I see something
different. That at least is consistent. (*To* JOAN) Are you ready?

JOAN
You'll come with me to see the Emperor?

ABE
Now comes an Emperor.

COHN
She and I have a mission!

JOAN
(*To* ABE)
And you too.

ABE
Me? I'm dead.

JOAN
You won't come with us?

ABE
I beg your pardon. Two's company, three's a crowd.

COHN
Look, are we going to go or are we going to stay here and argue?

ABE
I don't want to keep you.

JOAN
(*Confused*)
I'm not sure I should leave you.

COHN
Joan—any time you're ready.

ABE

Twenty years, Cohn, and now you go outside.

COHN

I'm not rigid!

ABE

You've changed!

COHN

Is that a crime?

ABE

(*Deeply disturbed*)

It's—it's a miracle! (*To* JOAN) To change Cohn—to make him move an inch, not to mention he goes outside, is nothing less than a miracle. Who are you?

JOAN

I told you.

ABE

(*Stares at her for a long time.*)

It's possible.

JOAN

Then you'll come?

ABE

Impossible.

JOAN

You have to come!

COHN

You can't stay here alone.

ABE

I'll manage.

COHN

Who'll cook for you?

ABE
I'll learn.

COHN
You won't learn.

ABE
Then I won't learn.

COHN
You'll starve.

ABE
It's possible. But unlikely.

COHN
(*To* JOAN)
I don't have all day, you know.

JOAN
We must go.
(*Opens front door.* COHN *goes out.*)

COHN
Hey, it's not so bad!

(JOAN *takes a long, sad look at* ABE.)

FIRST VOICE
Joan—

JOAN
(*Freezes.*)
Yes.

ABE
What's that?

SECOND VOICE
You can't leave.

ABE
Who said that?

JOAN
But my mission—

FIRST VOICE
Your mission is to take two of every kind.

ABE
(*Looks around.*)
Who said that?

JOAN
I know.

FIRST VOICE
That includes schlepps.

ABE
(*Still looking.*)
Who said that?

FIRST VOICE
You need one more.

(ABE *walks around looking for the* VOICES. JOAN *moves away from the door, back into the room.* COHN *appears in the doorway.*)

COHN
Well?

(*Nobody moves.*)

CURTAIN

Act Two

(*A month later. The house is no less cramped but much more orderly, like a military barracks. The screen has been moved from the kitchen to a corner near the bedrooms, where it partially hides a sloppily made army cot, in which* COHN *presently sleeps. Lying across the foot of the cot is a violin, several cookbooks, and the Bible.* COHN *sits in his chair at the oak table. His head is bowed, his hands clasped, praying.* ABE *comes out of his bedroom, obviously ill at ease in* COHN's *presence. He crosses to the typewriter, stares at the nearly blank sheet, and punches a key.* COHN *looks up.* ABE, *refusing to meet his eyes, turns and disappears into his room.* COHN *looks heavenward.*)

COHN

God? Cohn again. How long? That's all I ask. The main thing is the waiting. How important in the scheme of things, one Abe more or less. The suffering I don't mind. In fact, so far it's minimal; to be frank, nonexistent; to tell you the truth, a pleasure. But if I had to, believe me, suffering! Sacrifice! You say the word, it's a commitment. For that girl—*and* you—it's you name it! (JOAN *enters from* COHN's *bedroom.* COHN *jumps up in embarrassment.*) Speak of the devil!

JOAN

How proud of you I am, Cohn.

COHN

You're proud, I'm proud, we're both proud. You changed my life.

JOAN

Not I. God.

COHN

You first. You gave me proof. Tangibles.

JOAN

Faith is the absence of proof.

COHN

Still, it needs a beginning.

JOAN

From within!

COHN

You want something to eat? I have on a veal loaf. It'll be ready in no time. First start with this.
(*Hands her a plate of antipasto.*)

JOAN

I shouldn't, really. It's delicious.

COHN

Eat. (*Watches her eat.*) You take small bites for a soldier.

JOAN

I can't help but think of all those who go hungry.

COHN

Soon that will end. (JOAN *plows into her food.*) It *will* end soon, won't it?

JOAN

(*Eating compulsively.*)
What?

COHN
Hunger. Famine.

JOAN
When?

COHN
When?!

JOAN
(*In mid-bite*)
Oh, heaven! You mean heaven! Of course! (*Resumes eating.*)
I'm sorry, this is so delicious that I—(*Puts plate down.*)

COHN
No. Finish. Finish.

JOAN
(*Hesitates.*)
God's will be done. I am his servant.
(*Resumes eating passionately. A warm exchange of stares.* ABE
enters, sees COHN *and* JOAN *together, starts to back-pedal to his
room.* JOAN *spots him and rises.*)

ABE
I beg your pardon. (*Crosses to stove as if crossing a mine field.*)
I'll be out of your way in a minute. (*Pours himself a cup of
coffee. With sudden resentment*) Far be it for me to make a pest
of myself.

JOAN
(*Starts toward him.*)
Abe—

ABE
(*Circles around her.*)
Abe's my name. Invisibility's my game.
(*Disappears behind his curtain.*)

JOAN
He won't let me talk to him.

COHN
(*Sullen*)
That's his problem.

JOAN
Our problem!

(ABE, *his collar raised so as to make him invisible, slinks out again.*)

ABE
I'm not even here.

(ABE *crosses to the refrigerator and takes out a container of milk. On his way back* JOAN *plants herself in his path.* ABE *stops, turns, and starts back to the refrigerator. He opens it and sticks his head in as far as it will go, pretending to look for something.* JOAN *comes up behind him and stands there.* ABE *retreats even farther into the refrigerator, until more of him is in than out. Through it all* COHN *sits and glowers, jealous of the attention* ABE *is getting.*)

JOAN
May I say something, Abe? (*A long wait.*) I'd like to speak to you. (JOAN *does not move.* ABE *does not move. Finally he sneezes. Instinctively,* JOAN *puts a hand on his shoulder.*) Abe—

(ABE *reacts as if he's been shot. His head jerks up against the roof of the fridge with a resounding clunk. Stunned, his entire body, or what we see of it, sags. If we can see his head, it now lies on the first shelf.* JOAN *drags him out, closes the door, and half carries him to his chair.*)

ABE
I never felt better.

JOAN
Abe, why won't you speak to me? (ABE *doesn't answer.*) I've been here for weeks and we haven't exchanged a dozen words.

ABE
A dozen eggs?

JOAN
A dozen words.

ABE
What do you want to exchange a dozen words for? Are they
dirty? How do I know you even bought them here?

JOAN
You confuse me, Abe.

ABE
Confusme. That's a Chinese philosopher.

JOAN
That's Confucius.

ABE
Confucius is a color.

JOAN
That's fuchsia.

ABE
Fuchsia is what you say when there's a bad smell.

JOAN
That's phew.

ABE
Phew is a body of water in Norway.

JOAN
That's fjord.

ABE
Fjord is a car.

JOAN
That's Ford.

ABE

Ford is the number after three.

JOAN

That's four.

ABE

What's four?

JOAN

A number!

ABE

Absolutely right, I was so cold I was number. (*Rises.*) It's a pleasure finally talking to you.

(*He staggers on the run into his room.* JOAN *looks after him, then turns to* COHN, *who all this while has been glaring sullenly at the scene. He turns away from her.* JOAN *crosses to him.*)

JOAN

Tell me what to do, Cohn.

COHN

(*Brusque*)

Forget it.

JOAN

(*Squeezes his shoulder.*)

God depends on you, Cohn.

COHN

God? (*He rises, very haughtily.*) Sometimes, very frankly, it's hard to take some of this stuff seriously.

(COHN *walks past her into the kitchen and busies himself at the stove.* JOAN *crosses to darkened window, looks out.*)

JOAN

(*Softly*)

Voices? I see signs. I think it's going well. (*Looks around with some anxiety.*) Voices!?

FIRST VOICE
What now?

SECOND VOICE
Yes, Joan.

JOAN
I'm really very encouraged.

FIRST VOICE
She's encouraged.

SECOND VOICE
It doesn't take much.

JOAN
I have faith! They are almost ready.

SECOND VOICE
Joan—

FIRST VOICE
What are we going to do with her?

JOAN
I don't understand. Don't you think things are going well? Cohn is with me, that's one . . .

SECOND VOICE
I'll say he's one.

JOAN
And now that Abe is talking to me—

SECOND VOICE
Joan, come to your senses.

JOAN
Didn't you see it? *He is talking to me!*

SECOND VOICE
Talk to her.

FIRST VOICE
You talk to her.

SECOND VOICE
Who can talk to her? You talk to her.

FIRST VOICE
I don't want to talk to her. Frankly, I'm heartsick.

JOAN
What in the world is wrong with you today, Voices?

SECOND VOICE
Will you listen to the mouth on her?

FIRST VOICE
(*Warning*)
Take it back, Joan!

JOAN
(*Fearful*)
I'm unworthy! I take it back! (*Pause. Confused*) What?

FIRST VOICE
She doesn't know.

SECOND VOICE
Hopeless.

JOAN
What? Am I displeasing you? I thought everything was wonderful.
(*Grabs for her plate, eats compulsively.*)

SECOND VOICE
Stuffs herself like a pig.

FIRST VOICE
Any second now—crash!—armor all over the place.

JOAN
Why are you so angry with me? (*Hesitates in her eating. Reluctantly puts down plate.*) I am the servant of the Lord. I do his bidding.

FIRST VOICE
Will you look at her complexion? Breaking out.

SECOND VOICE
And why not? She hasn't been out of the house in a month.

FIRST VOICE
I think that you are losing your faith, Joan.

JOAN
Never!

SECOND VOICE
Not five minutes ago you forgot about heaven.

JOAN
Not for a second!

FIRST VOICE
Admit it! When you were eating.

JOAN
It slipped my mind for one second. Is that a mortal sin?

SECOND VOICE
Are you questioning us?

JOAN
I'm asking—

SECOND VOICE
Questioning!

JOAN
Not seriously—

SECOND VOICE
Losing faith.

JOAN
I have faith!

SECOND VOICE
Faith to do what?

JOAN
To believe!

SECOND VOICE
Believe in what?

JOAN
Believe in my Voices!

FIRST VOICE
We don't want you to say it if you don't mean it.

JOAN
With all my heart and soul! Before my Voices what was I? But with my Voices who am I? Do you think I can overlook such change? But it's so hard. Cohn, no matter what I say, he will agree. But to what end? No end. And Abe hates me. I know he hates me. Why should he hate me?

FIRST VOICE
Nobody said it would be easy.

SECOND VOICE
You must strengthen your faith. Strong faith sweeps all before it.

FIRST VOICE
Faith can move mountains, Joan.

JOAN
Voices! Let me go to a mountain!

SECOND VOICE
Joan, your trial is here.

JOAN
I beg of you, let me first move a mountain.

FIRST VOICE
Can you believe this?

JOAN
I promise, Voices, I shall make good on a mountain; then I shall return here.

FIRST VOICE
Hopeless!

SECOND VOICE
Admit it, we picked a real lemon this time.

(JOAN *whirls as a rock crashes through the window and lands at her feet.* COHN *and* ABE *come running. All stare down at the rock.* JOAN *stoops to pick it up.*)

COHN
Don't touch!

ABE
It's an animal!

COHN
It's a bomb!

ABE
It's not a bomb.

COHN
It's not an animal.

(JOAN *reaches for it.*)

ABE and COHN
Don't pick it up!
(JOAN *picks it up.*)

JOAN
It's a rock.

COHN
Get it away! Away! I hear ticking!

ABE
There's writing on it.

COHN
(*Scornfully to* ABE)
Who writes on rocks?

ABE
(*Scornfully to* COHN)
Who writes on bombs?

COHN
(*A wave of dismissal.*)
Later!

JOAN
It's a message!

COHN
Don't read it!

ABE
Who writes on rocks? It says—

JOAN
(*Reading*)
"You will meet new challenges, which can be turned into opportunities. Beware of January, February, and March."

COHN
(*Crosses to window. Shouts.*)
Get away from here! This is no time for jokes!

(*A knock at the door. All jump.* JOAN *goes to the door. An aged, stooped* MESSENGER *in a cap.*)

MESSENGER (WISEMAN)
I have a rock for Joan of Arc.

JOAN

I'll take it.

MESSENGER

You Joan of Arc? (JOAN *nods.*) Sign here, please. (JOAN *signs his pad. He hands her the rock, then stares at her.*) You really Joan of Arc?

JOAN

I am.

MESSENGER

(Begins to chuckle and shake his head.) Joan of Arc.

(JOAN gently closes the door on the chuckling MESSENGER. *She reads the rock.*)

JOAN

"Beware of April, May, and June." (*With a loud squeal, the refrigerator door swings open.* JOAN, COHN, *and* ABE *look up. A rock falls out of the refrigerator.* JOAN *drops the second rock and crosses to the new rock. She kneels and reads it.*) "Also July, August, September, October, November, December."

ABE

That's it as far as I'm concerned.

(He goes on the run into his bedroom. COHN *crosses to the door.*)

COHN

(Whispers.) While it's still dark, let's make a break.

JOAN

Not without Abe.

COHN

(Fed up) Abe?! Who knows what's out there?

JOAN
And I believed you had faith.

COHN
(*Conspiratorial*)
You want Abe? (*Takes drug off stock shelf.*) A pinch of this in Abe's soup. In no time, out like a baby. I guarantee after twenty years inside, we get him outside. He won't leave our side.

JOAN
(*Disbelieving*)
You want me to trick Abe?

COHN
Tactics. You never heard of tactics? All right, you don't like pharmacology, here's plan two: While he was inside hiding, he missed a second messenger. A Hollywood offer. Big money. A documentary. A movie pilgrimage to the Emperor. Trust me, if Abe falls for it, we can handle the others.

JOAN
(*Puzzled*)
You want me to fool Abe?

COHN
Who wouldn't want to be in pictures? They'll fall for it, two of every kind. I guarantee: a cast of thousands.

JOAN
(*Shocked*)
You want me to lie?

COHN
First and last we remember the mission. Later is time enough for the truth.

JOAN
From the beginning!

COHN
The beginning's too soon for unorganized truth. It needs preparation. You don't like movies? Here's plan three: We'll say we're

the police, charges have been made but it's a free country. They'll have their day in court, they should come with us to appeal before the Emperor.

JOAN

Cohn, what's come over you?

COHN

You give them a little fear, they get a move on. No dilly-dally. No explanations. The main thing is the mission.

JOAN

You actually want me to lie!

COHN

It's no bed of roses out there. In me, you're fortunate to find a man of imagination, but out there, you tell them you're Joan of Arc, I guarantee it's no laugh riot.

JOAN

They will believe me.

COHN

What? Two bricklayers? Two carpenters? Two truck drivers? Two taxi drivers? Two advertising-agency executives? Joan. Joan, what am I going to do with you? It's a whirlpool you're walking into. Not even you can walk on whirlpools. It takes fiddling. A story here. A little piece of business there. You maneuver. You manipulate. Push comes to shove, a wheel, a deal, we got ourselves an army. Trust me.

JOAN

I trust God.

COHN

No argument. No argument. He gives policy, I carry it out. Where's the contradiction?

JOAN

I trust my Voices.

COHN

Voices always have to be right? Believe me, Joan, I've worked this out.

JOAN

Believe you? I can scarcely believe my senses!

COHN

Voices talk, they don't listen. They're Voices. What do they know? Two of every kind. Abe and me? Never! Not in a million years! Even superficially—Glutton. Gourmet. If they could see they'd know.

JOAN

They do know.

COHN

I can make a mistake, you can make a mistake. Voices can't make mistakes? That's not in the realm of possibility?

JOAN

How can you have faith and still question?

COHN

I don't question.

JOAN

Cohn, has questioning ever given you satisfaction?

COHN

The opposite. I don't question.

JOAN

Has it ever made you happy?

COHN

Not once. I don't question.

JOAN

Do you believe I am Joan?

COHN

Yes.

JOAN
Do you believe in my mission?

COHN
Yes!

JOAN
Do you believe the sky is missing?

COHN
Yes! Yes! Yes!

JOAN
Praise the Lord!

COHN
Praise the Lord!

JOAN
(*Takes his hand.*)
You are my right hand, Cohn.

COHN
(*Falls to his knees, clasps her hands.*)
You want to know who's two of the same kind, not Abe and me,
you and me! More than that is a complication. Do we need it?
In my opinion: no. Travel fast, travel light. We go it alone!
Trust me!

(*He strides to the door and throws it open. A* SOLDIER *in combat
dress, wearing a gas mask and carrying an automatic rifle, stands
in the doorway.* COHN, *still staring at* JOAN *does not see him. He
holds his hand out, beckoning her to the great outdoors. His
hand brushes against the* SOLDIER'S *gas mask. He turns, very
slowly, to see what he's touching, sees, and slams shut the door.
A siren sounds. The room is flooded with searchlights.*)

POLICE VOICE (WISEMAN)
(*Miked*)
Send out the girl! We only want the girl!

ABE
(*Crawling out of his room on his belly.*)
I knew it!

POLICE VOICE
We don't want you. We only want the girl.

JOAN
I'll go!

COHN
(*Stops her.*)
No!

ABE
(*Shouts.*)
You can have her! You can have her!

COHN
(*To* ABE)
You go!

ABE
Ah hah! Didn't I know it?!

POLICE VOICE
We don't want Abe, we want the girl.

JOAN
Let me speak to them!

COHN
They're your enemies.

JOAN
I have no enemies.

ABE
She has no enemies, let her go.

COHN
(*Restraining* JOAN.)
No! *I'll* go!

POLICE VOICE
We don't want Cohn, we want the girl.

COHN
(*Shouts.*)
It's all or nothing! You want her, you got to kill us all!

ABE
All? What all?!

POLICE VOICE
We don't want to kill you all, we only want to kill the girl.

COHN
(*To* JOAN)
See?

JOAN
They won't harm me. They are my army!

COHN
Are you crazy? You're Joan of Arc! They want to burn you at the stake!

JOAN
Voices!

POLICE VOICE
Yes?

JOAN
I want *my* Voices!

POLICE VOICE
The game's up, sister. Throw out your armor and come out with your hands up!

JOAN
He's drowning out my Voices!

POLICE VOICE
(*Croons.*)
I dream of Joanie
With the light blond hair,
Floating like a vapor
On the soft, summer air.

(*As* POLICE VOICE *sings,* ABE *leaps into the trunk and pulls the lid down over him.* COHN *dashes for the bedroom and comes out with his shotgun.* JOAN, *at the door, tries to pull it open. It is locked. She fiddles with the bolt. By this time,* COHN *is at the window and fires a blast.*) Very nice! (*A white flag is poked through the shattered window.*) Don't shoot. I'm coming in to parley.

(*The door opens.* JOAN *leaps back. In walks* WISEMAN, *in robes as before, but with a silver star pinned to his chest. He crosses to the table, sits, puts on a green eyeshade, and begins shuffling a deck of cards.* COHN *backs off in horror.*)

WISEMAN
To make it interesting we play for the girl. (*Looks at them.*) Who plays?

(*Stares at* COHN, *who backs into the trunk.* ABE *lifts the lid and peers out at* WISEMAN. *He climbs out of the trunk as* COHN *climbs in and pulls shut the lid.* ABE *crosses to* WISEMAN *and sits.*)

ABE
We play for peace and quiet.

WISEMAN
I win, I get the girl; you win, you get peace and quiet. (*He deals the cards. They study their hands. As each discards, he calls out his card.*) Fifty-five.

ABE
Seventy-one.

WISEMAN
King.

ABE.
Einstein.

WISEMAN
Queen.

ABE
Garbo.

WISEMAN
Jack.

ABE
Daniel's.

WISEMAN
One.

ABE
Meatball.

WISEMAN
Ashtray.

ABE
Match.

WISEMAN
Deuce.

ABE
Game.

WISEMAN
Loophole.

ABE
Manhole.

WISEMAN
Fix.

ABE
Parking ticket.

WISEMAN
Horse.

ABE
Fire engine.

WISEMAN
Love.

ABE
Stock market.

WISEMAN
Cadillac.

ABE
Morphine.

WISEMAN
Mortuary.

ABE
February.

WISEMAN
Wake.

ABE
Corn flakes.

WISEMAN
Banco!

ABE
Bunko!

WISEMAN
(*Fans out his cards.*)
An inside straight!

ABE
(*Fans out his cards.*)
An outside patio with a rose garden!

(WISEMAN *growls, kicks over his chair, and storms out.*)

JOAN
(*Crosses to* ABE.)
You are a wonderful card player.

(ABE *doesn't look at her. He shuffles the cards.* JOAN *sits next to him.* ABE *continues to shuffle.*)

ABE
I'll give you the answer, you give me the question. Chicken teriyaki.

JOAN
I don't understand.

ABE
I'll give you the answer. You give me the question. It's a game.

JOAN
Oh.

ABE
Chicken teriyaki. (JOAN *looks at him nonplused.*) You don't know? The question is: Who is the oldest living kamikaze pilot? Here's another: Nine-W. (JOAN *doesn't respond.*) Now you give me the question.

JOAN
I wasn't listening.

ABE

The answer is nine-W. What's the question?

JOAN

I don't know.

ABE

The question is: Do you spell your name with a "V," Herr Wagner? You ready for another?

(JOAN *reaches out to him.*)

JOAN

Abe—

(ABE *pulls away. A pause.*)

ABE

All right, here's another. The answer is: From birth, I was taught to believe: Where there's a will there's a way. But nobody wrote me into his will, so I had to make my own way. Still, I had hope. Someday I would find the right situation. In the meantime, I piled up money. For when I found the right situation. Also I married. A mistake, but bearable. It didn't take too much of either of our time. Whenever we exchanged understanding stares, I found out later it was a misunderstanding. So I wondered: Is this all? I couldn't accept yes for an answer, so I left my wife and I started looking. She sent Cohn to bring me back. Instead, he talked me into looking where he wanted to look instead of where I wanted. Finally, we split up. I went on looking. High and low, inside and out, until I got so depressed I couldn't hold my head up. So not being able to hold my head up, I saw straight in front of me for the first time. And looking right in my face was the answer. In life you don't look too high and you don't look too low, you look straight down the middle. The answer lies in the middle. In the middle there's always room for hope and not too much room for disappointment. So the lesson of life is to settle. So I came to the woods. To settle. I found this house, I knocked on the door and Cohn opened it. He had settled the year before me. It's not terrific. But also it's not painful. I don't hurt anybody. It's an across-the-board settlement. I don't love it, I don't hate it. That's the answer, what's the question?

JOAN

The question is: If you want to believe in something, can't you come up with anything better than that?

(*They continue to stare at each other.*)

ABE

I beg your pardon. (*Rises, looks at typewriter, punches a key, looks at paper, pulls it out, and crumples it.*) I'll put it this way. I'll start. How far I get is another question.

JOAN
(*Slowly realizing*)
You'll go? You'll come?

ABE
(*Smiles.*)
I'll accompany.
(*Backs off into his doorway, where he lingers for a moment, then disappears.*)

JOAN

You'll accompany! You'll accompany! Cohn! (*Looks for him.*) Abe will accompany! (COHN *lifts the lid of the trunk an inch or two and peers out.*) Abe will accompany! He'll accompany!

ABE

(*Pokes his head out from behind his curtain.*)
Miss? Joan? Could you possibly—

(JOAN *charges through* ABE'*s curtain.* COHN *stands up in the trunk and looks after her.*)

COHN

He'll change his mind! I know him!

JOAN
(*Pokes her head out from behind curtain.*)
He's beginning to pack!
(*Ducks back in.*)

COHN

It's a lie! He's lying!

JOAN
(*Pokes her head out.*)
He's packing! He's actually packing!
(*Ducks back in.*)

COHN

I've been through this before!

JOAN
(*Pokes her head out.*)
Do you know where he put his muffler? He won't go outside
without his muffler!
(*Back in.*)

COHN

He's backing down!

JOAN
(*Head out.*)
He found his muffler!
(*Back in.*)

COHN

It's the wrong muffler!

JOAN
(*Head out.*)
He's packed!
(*Back in.*)

COHN

He's not to be trusted!

JOAN

(*Head out.*)
He's putting on his galoshes!
(*Back in.*)

COHN

We can't wait! He'll slow us down!

JOAN

(*Head out.*)
He's coming!

COHN

We'll never get there!

JOAN

(*Throws open curtain and introduces* ABE.)
He's *here*!
(ABE *emerges past* JOAN, *bandaged in winter clothes, lugging a huge suitcase.*)

ABE

What a sensational day for a trip!

JOAN

Onward to the Emperor!

FIRST VOICE

Onward to the Emperor!

SECOND VOICE

Onward to the Emperor!

(ABE *and* JOAN *move to the door.* JOAN *throws open the door.* COHN *disappears into the trunk and slams shut the lid.* ABE *and* JOAN *stand waiting.*)

COHN

(*Raises the lid one-half inch.*)
You know what you can do with those buttinsky, wiseacre Voices of yours? I *wish* you never heard of them! You know what I *wish*—I *wish* you never heard of Joan of Arc!
(*Slams shut the lid. Light and music effect.*)

JOAN

(*Puts on bandanna cap, grabs broom, starts sweeping. Turns to* ABE.)
Abe, what are you all bundled up for? (*Starts unwrapping him.*)
You're not going out in this weather. After dark? In the night air? Without your dinner? Cohn, can you imagine? Honestly! You two!

(*She continues to unbundle the stunned* ABE. COHN *stands up in the trunk and looks on.*)

CURTAIN

Act Three

(Five months later. The House is as cramped as before and far more disorganized. Everything looks as if it's been moved and for no particular purpose. Altogether the impression is of impending chaos. JOAN's tarnished armor hangs in sections on several hooks of a clothes tree. It is dinnertime. Two pots on the stove give off lots of steam. The dining-room table is littered with dirty dishes. ABE's typewriter and stacks of paper are nowhere in sight. ABE comes out from behind his curtained doorway wearing a bathrobe, carrying a half-empty glass of milk. He brushes past JOAN's armor.)

ABE

In the way. As usual.

(He stops, scowls at the armor, then tentatively touches it. He takes the headpiece off its hook, is about to try it on when JOAN rises out of the steam from behind the kitchen counter. She wears an old-fashioned, long flowered dress and a frilly apron. Her complexion is pale and waxen.)

JOAN
(Excited)
Almost ready!

(She lifts the cover off a pot, burns her hand on the handle, and lets go with a loud scream. The cover flies across the room through COHN's *curtained doorway.* COHN *rushes out, holding pot cover. He is a nervous, contrite, less abrasive* COHN)

COHN
Joan—

JOAN
(Whirls on him.)
Stay put!

COHN
(Freezes.)
But—

JOAN
If it didn't belong there I wouldn't have thrown it there! *(Turns back to stove.)* One more minute!

COHN
(Not daring to move.)
It smells delicious!

ABE
(Crosses to table and sits.)
It was one more minute fifteen minutes ago.

JOAN
Cooking one thing at a time is no problem, it's cooking combinations.

ABE
If excuses were only edible.

COHN
(To ABE, *placating)*
She's trying.

ABE
If reasons were raisins I wouldn't go hungry.

JOAN
(*Whirls on* ABE.)
What did you say?

ABE
Me? Not a word.

JOAN
(*Turns back to stove.*)
The trick is to get the roast and the beans and the cauliflower
and the potatoes all done at the same—I think it's ready.

(*Opens the oven door. Thick black smoke spurts out, darkening*
JOAN's *face and sending her into a fit of coughing. She grabs a*
dish towel and covers her face. Staggering around, she backs into
the stove and knocks the pots off.)

COHN
(*Alarmed*)
Careful!

(JOAN *manages to escape the downpour of boiling water and*
vegetables. In her jumping about she sends the spice shelf flying.
In her attempt to regain her balance, she flails out and grabs hold
of the bottom shelf of the dish cabinet. The shelf gives way and
all the dishes descend on her. JOAN *disappears from view under a*
pile of debris. COHN *leans forward tensely,* ABE *leans back, con-*
temptuous.)

ABE
Typical.

(COHN *starts toward the kitchen.*)

JOAN
(*Out of sight.*)
Everyone stay out of here. (COHN *keeps coming. He gets to the*
kitchen. JOAN *screams.*) *Stay out!* I had a little accident. No
one's hurt. (*Snarls to* COHN) Everything's under control.

COHN
(*Advances a step.*)
Let me—

JOAN
(*Screams.*)
I don't need help! (*Rises from the floor, her hair in disarray, her blouse ripped, but with a blackened roast pig on a platter, an apple in its mouth. She marches proudly to the dining table and slams down the platter.*) No vegetables tonight. (*Glares at* COHN.) All right?

COHN
(*Feigned cheerfulness*)
Fine.

JOAN
(*Glares at* ABE.)
All right?

ABE
I had vegetables yesterday.

(COHN *starts carving the pig.* JOAN *goes back to the kitchen and begins sweeping up the wreckage. It makes a terrific clatter.*)

COHN
Don't you want to eat, Joan?

JOAN
(*Snaps.*)
Later.

COHN
Don't you at least want to sit with us?

JOAN
(*Snaps.*)
Later.
(COHN *sighs and starts eating.*)

ABE

A terrific companion. If she wasn't so handy around the kitchen, I'd suggest we get rid of her.

COHN

(*Low*)

She hasn't been well.

ABE

(*Picks up a charred slice of pig.*)

Look at that. By what stretch of the imagination could this possibly be called food?

COHN

It's not bad.

ABE

This is a pig not even a pig would eat.

COHN

A little charity!

ABE

You want charity? Ask the Emperor!

JOAN

(*Recoils suddenly, as if in reaction to* ABE's *harsh reminder.*)

Ouch!

COHN

(*Jumps up.*)

What happened?

JOAN

Nothing.

COHN

(*In fear*)

You cut yourself!

JOAN

It's all right.

ABE
(*To* COHN)
Stop making a fool of yourself. Sit down.

COHN
Let me look!

JOAN
Stay put. It's only a cut finger.

COHN
Oh my God!

JOAN
(*Comes out of the kitchen, one finger aloft.*)
Oh, stop it, Cohn. Nobody dies of a cut finger.

(*She faints dead away.* COHN *runs to her, scoops her up in his arms, and carries her to the couch. He empties the couch of its litter and lays* JOAN *down.*)

COHN
Abe, quick! Bandages! Gauze! Iodine! Brandy! (ABE *leans back in his chair, stretches his arms, and yawns.*) Heartless!

ABE
She's faking.

COHN
Heartless! Heartless!

ABE
I know a faker when I see it. You talk heaven to her, she burns a pig; talk mission, she cuts a finger; talk going outside, she falls asleep. Free room and board. In exchange for what? Minnie the Moocher. In my life among bad deals I include this with the worst.

COHN
She's dying!

ABE

She fainted. I died. And believe you me, I didn't get all this attention. (COHN *rushes off for medical equipment.* ABE *strolls
over to* JOAN.) All right. Have it your way for now. I'm patient.
Nobody outwaits Abe. I only get fooled once. A stranger cries
"Heaven!" You take a look. It's only polite, what could it hurt?
If it turns out heaven, so much the better. If not, what's to lose?
One more disappointment. In my life that's hardly an event. I
worked on Wall Street thirty years, but for hope I was ready to
take a plunge. So what do I get for my investment? People jump
out of the window for less.

(COHN *rushes back in.* ABE *walks back to the table.*)

COHN
(*On his knees beside* JOAN)
The bleeding stopped. Look how white she is, Abe.

ABE
(*Indicates door.*)
She's free to get all the air she wants. With my blessing.

COHN
You're upset, that's why you're talking that way.

ABE
Me? Do I look upset?
(*He doesn't.*)

COHN
(*Eager to make up*)
I apologize for calling you heartless. It was a moment of excite-
ment.

ABE
Who listened?

COHN
'(*Confidential*)
Listen, while she's out, you want me to make you a little some-
thing?

ABE

I'm not hungry.

COHN

An omelet? You love my omelets.

ABE

I'm full. On pig.

COHN

You name it, I'll cook it.

ABE

Don't trouble yourself.

COHN

Trouble? It would be a pleasure.

ABE

Thank you, but food no longer interests me.

COHN

She's breathing more regular. (JOAN *wakes*.) Stay still.

JOAN
(*Sullen*)

That's easy enough for you to say.

COHN

What's so important you can't rest a minute?

JOAN

The kitchen.

COHN

I can't clean it up?

JOAN

I don't want you in my kitchen.

COHN

I won't go near it.

JOAN
Stop humoring me.

COHN
I'm only trying to be friends.

JOAN
I have no friends.

COHN
I'm not a friend?

JOAN
You say it but you don't mean it.

COHN
I mean it with my heart.

JOAN
Abe's not my friend.

COHN
Abe is crazy about you.

JOAN
He hates me. And you're his friend, so you must hate me.

COHN
Abe loves you, I love you. You're a little sick so you feel bad.

JOAN
He makes me feel useless. He's the one who's useless. If I ever get
my health back, I'm going to tell him that. He's right. I am useless. I mess up everything. I don't blame him for not liking me.
Sometimes I hate you.

COHN
(*Hurt*)
Don't worry about it.

JOAN
I bore you.

COHN
You don't!

JOAN
I bore me, so I must bore you.

COHN
The other way around.

JOAN
You mean I bore Abe too?

COHN
I mean I bore you.

JOAN
You do bore me.

COHN
(*Fearful*)
You want to leave!

JOAN
You want me to leave.

COHN
You're bored and you want to leave.

JOAN
I don't want to leave.

COHN
Why shouldn't you?

JOAN
I'll go if you want me to.

COHN
Never!

JOAN
Where would I go?

COHN
(*Upset*)
That's all that's keeping you. If you knew where to go, you'd be
out of here like a shot.

JOAN
(*Angry*)
I don't want to leave.

COHN
You're saying it to make me feel good.

JOAN
What could possibly be out there that I'd want?

COHN
(*Guilty*)
Nothing is out there! But if there was—

JOAN
But there isn't!

COHN
But you'd go!

JOAN
I don't care what there is—I wouldn't go.

COHN
I just want you to be happy.

JOAN
(*Helpless pause.*)
Well, I'm mostly happy.

COHN
(*Anxious*)
But you're sick.

JOAN
I'm much better.

COHN

You're weak. You take on too much. You should do less.

JOAN

If I did less I'd die.

COHN

(*Insistent*)

But you're happy. (JOAN *nods*.) Well, that's all I care about. If I could believe that, then I'd sleep easy.

JOAN

(*Frightened*)

Aren't you sleeping well?

COHN

I worry.

JOAN

I will never go.

COHN

So I won't worry.

(COHN *lays his head in her lap and starts humming a Mozart aria.* JOAN *moves* COHN's *head off her lap and stands. She takes two steps and falls into a dead faint.* COHN, *on the couch, continues humming and does not notice.* ABE *comes out of the kitchen, where he's been sneaking a cold meal out of the refrigerator. He stops and looks down at* JOAN.)

ABE

(*To* JOAN)

You should be an actress on the stage. (*Stares down at her while gnawing away at a chicken leg. Suddenly he bends down to take a closer look. He feels her pulse.*) She's dying.

COHN

She's happy.

(*Resumes humming.*)

ABE

(Listens to her heart.)
She's dead. (*Rises. To* COHN) You really did it this time.

(COHN *jumps up and runs to the fallen* JOAN. ABE *walks off.*)

COHN

Water! Smelling salts! Pepper! Garlic! Brandy! (*Shakes* JOAN'S
lifeless body.) I warned her to take it easy. But no, she has to
have her own way! (*Shakes her more violently*). She won't listen! (*Strokes her face.*) Pale like a ghost. (*Flutters a hand back
and forth across her face.*) She's not well enough to go out.
Wake up, Joan! (*Slaps her lightly.*) Abe, where's the water?
(*Looks up at* ABE, *who has not moved.*) What is this? Sadism?!
Cooperate!

ABE

It's over. You did it.

COHN

(*Shakes* JOAN, *slaps her face repeatedly, with increasing alarm.*)
Wake up! (*Shakes her.*) I get no cooperation!
(*Lifts her angrily and throws her on the couch.*)

ABE

Very nice.

COHN

(*Desperate*)
Not one ounce of cooperation from anyone around here. It's her
who's sick, not me, but does she help? Fat chance! No help!
Never helps! Just faints. Faints! Faints! Faints! You could clock
it on the hour. As if she has anything really wrong with her;
don't tell me! Hysterical reaction. Getting even. Childish! Childish! What did I do? What was my crime! Why all this torture!
If I'm a criminal, get it over, put me on trial!

(*Door flies open.* WISEMAN *enters in his robes, wearing a judge's
wig and carrying law books.*)

BAILIFF'S VOICE

Oyez! Oyez! The Second Hessian of the Fourth Circuit Court of the Fifth at Aqueduct is now inoperative. Judge Helmut Wiseman presiding.

WISEMAN

(*Uprights the trunk and bangs a gavel on it.*)
This court is now in session. Who represents the accursed—uh—accused?

ABE

I do, your honor.

WISEMAN

Who represents the prosecution?

ABE

I do, your honor.

COHN

So that's what you're up to! I knew it all the time! I wasn't born yesterday!

ABE

Your honor, the defendant alleges he wasn't boring yesterday.

WISEMAN

Is he aware he's under oath?

COHN

I'm not under oath. I'm not under anything!

ABE

If your honor pleases, I have an expert witness who will testify that the defendant was boring yesterday.

WISEMAN

Let me admonish the defendant of the danger of committing perjury.

ABE

Your honor, I have additional expert testimony which will prove that the defendant has been boring for twenty years; that, in fact, the defendant has a history of being boring to a point of tears, death, and distraction.

WISEMAN

(*Picks up imaginary phone.*)
Hello. Tears, Death, and Distraction. I'm sorry, Mr. Tears is dead, Mr. Death is distracted, and Mr. Distraction's in traction. I'll put you on to our Mr. Cohn. *Cohn!*

ABE

Take the stand!

WISEMAN

Do you swear to tell the truth, the whole truth, the half-truth, for better or worse, for whom the bell tolls, for me and my gal, in sickness, in health, in darkness, in light, in Newark, in Irvington, indecision, innuendo, so help you God?

COHN

Not on your life!

WISEMAN

Oh yeah?! Well, a knot on *your* life! (*Swings at* COHN's *head with the gavel.* COHN *ducks.* WISEMAN *falls off balance, over the trunk.*) Order! Did you hear me call for order?!

ABE

Fried eggs over light, with bacon.

WISEMAN

Toast?

ABE

(*Raises a glass.*)
To Joan of Arc.

WISEMAN

(*Stands, raises his gavel.*)
To Joan of Arc.

COHN

Ah ha! I gave you enough rope, you hung yourselves. I know your game! I admit nothing.

ABE

You admit you are Cohn?

COHN

I admit I tried. Can more be asked of any man?

ABE

And you were acquainted with this Joan of Arc?

COHN

She wasn't Joan of Arc!

ABE

I object, your honor. Giving adverse testimony about a deceased person who is in no position to defend herself.

COHN

She fainted. She's not dead. Who knows if she even fainted? (*Glares at them.*) Three of the same kind! I'm the one person here who can be trusted. *You* object? *I* object!

WISEMAN

Objections sustained.

ABE

I object!

WISEMAN

Objection sustained.

ABE

Where does that leave us?

WISEMAN

I object! Objection overruled! Are there any further questions to be asked of this witness?

ABE

Cohn, do you recognize this object?
(*Holds up* JOAN's *suit of armor.*)

COHN

It's a dress.

ABE

A dress. And do you recognize this object?
(*Holds up* JOAN's *sword.*)

COHN

It's a broom.

ABE

A dress and a broom. Mr. Cohn—(*Raises five fingers.*) Please identify what I am now holding up.

COHN

You want to know what you're holding up?

ABE

What am I holding up?

COHN

You're holding up these proceedings. (*Turns to* WISEMAN.) Ha!
(WISEMAN *bangs his gavel.*) You're all against me.

ABE

The judge is against you?

COHN

He's no judge. I know him from the old country.

ABE

I'm against you?

COHN

Tell me something I don't know.

ABE

The deceased was against you?

COHN

The worst of the lot. Look at her. I trusted her. The rest of you I knew better. You especially.

ABE

Me especially.

COHN

You especially.

ABE

Who pays for this house?

COHN

Every argument he brings it up. Move, I won't stop you.

ABE

It's my house!

COHN

I found it!

ABE

You rented. I bought!

COHN

So money makes everything all right? Is that the story? Plutocrat. Didn't I always know it? Plutocrat!

ABE

Nobody made you live with me.

COHN

I felt sorry for you. That's my weakness. Softness of heart. I took you in. I felt sorry for her, I took her in. So tell me, where's the gratitude? Him twenty years, her six months, I'm still wait-

ing. I won't hold my breath. I'm guilty all right, guilty of being
an innocent set loose in a world full of thieves. Cutthroats.
Ingrates. That's my crime. Never again.

WISEMAN

The defendant has pleaded guilty of being innocent. I sentence
him to hang by the neck until dead. (*To* COHN) You want to
appeal the sentence?

COHN

Drop dead.

WISEMAN

Appeal granted. Say thank you.

COHN

You could first cut my tongue out.

WISEMAN

Motion granted. (*Whips out scissors.*) Witness, do you have anything to say before I pass sentence?

COHN

No.

WISEMAN

Do you have anything to say before I pass out?

COHN

No.

WISEMAN

(*Rings a bell.*)
Recess!
(*Tips back in chair and falls to the floor, asleep.*)

COHN

(*Quietly, after a long pause*)
I hope you're satisfied.

ABE

I didn't start it.

COHN
We were made fools of.

ABE
Not me.

COHN
You too.

ABE
You first!

COHN
You were of no help whatsoever!

ABE
Help *you?* You've got a mind like a closed fist. Who can argue with it? You believed that she heard voices!

COHN
I didn't!

ABE
You told me so yourself!

COHN
A metaphor!

ABE
You believed she had a mission.

COHN
No.

ABE
Yes.

COHN
Never!

ABE
Always!

COHN

Sometimes. Never always. Not even when I said it.

ABE

So why did you say it? (COHN *shrugs*.) To get back at me, that's why!

COHN

You?

ABE

So she'd like you better!

COHN

She *did* like me better.

ABE

Because you knew her first. Do you deny you told me she was Joan of Arc?

COHN

(*Evasive*)

I don't remember. (ABE *turns away in disgust*.) A charming conceit. Did it do harm? (*Improvising desperately*) She was cute. I liked her. She was nice—in my opinion—who knows? I wanted to please her. Pleasing a pretty girl. Is that so out of the question? I did it as a favor. A little game. A flirtation. Who understands women? I thought, in time, with patience, with understanding, the power of logic, I could talk her out of it.

ABE

You *wished* her out of it.

COHN

I didn't wish! (*A confession*) So I wished. You never wished?

ABE

You killed her!

COHN

Liar!!

ABE

You!

COHN

Killed her? Killed her? What are you saying? What a thing to say. I loved her! I believed in her? Killed her? Before her, I'd kill myself! (*Rushes over to* JOAN *and picks her up in his arms.*) The one person in this world who gave me anything! You gave me joy, I gave you doubt! You gave me hope, I gave you despondency! You gave me a second chance! And what did I do with it? What I did with my whole life! (*Overwhelming guilt*) I killed! I'm a killer! I should be killed. Locked up till I learn my lesson! (*Flash of insight*) I can't learn! I never learned! Never! Never! Never! (*Staggers over to* ABE.) Don't deny it, Abe, you're a saint! A saint! How could you put up with it? (*Embraces* ABE.) A man's best friend! (*Whips out a pistol.*) Kill me! Shoot me! (ABE *shoots—and misses. He blows a big hole in the back wall. Sunlight pours in.* COHN *and* ABE *squint in the sudden light.* JOAN *is bathed in light. She sits up slowly, rubbing her eyes.* COHN *does not see her. To* ABE) Idiot! Numskull! Can't you do anything right? (*Grabs pistol from* ABE *and turns it on himself.*)

JOAN

Cohn!

(JOAN's *cry causes* COHN's *hand to jerk at the moment of fire. A great hole is blown in the side wall. Sunlight pours in.* COHN *whirls on* JOAN, *drops the gun, and falls to his knees beside her. He covers his face with his hands and weeps.* JOAN *strokes his head.*)

COHN

A miracle! An angel from heaven!

JOAN

No, it's only me.

COHN

Say you forgive me.

JOAN
For what?

COHN
(*Angry*)
Never mind for what! Say it! (*In self-reproach*) I did it again!
(*Starts banging his head.*) Dog! Vermin! Pestilence!

JOAN
(Gently)
Cohn—(COHN *looks up.* JOAN *rises from couch, shakily.*) I must
leave you.

COHN
What are you saying?

JOAN
Farewell.

COHN
You're too sick to go out. It's freezing out there. Snow. Rain.
Sit. Rest.

JOAN
Farewell, Abe.

ABE
More tricks?

COHN
Don't go! I deserve it, but don't!

JOAN
Abe, can you ever forgive me?

ABE
What's to forgive?

JOAN
You hate me.

ABE
Who hates? I'm objective.

JOAN
You're angry with me.

ABE
Anger is a waste. I'm objective.

JOAN
You're disappointed in me.

ABE
Disappointment is subjective. I'm objective.

JOAN
Abe, I'm sorry. I must go. Something is calling me.

COHN
Nothing! What? Something?

JOAN
—something inside—

COHN
Calling you?

JOAN
Inside. Something.

COHN
Voices?

JOAN
No. Yes! Voices! Oh, Cohn, how did you know?

COHN
I have to hear!

JOAN
How can you hear what's inside me?

COHN
Don't cut me out, Joan! I'm a dying man.

JOAN

I'm a dying woman.

COHN

Don't compete. (*Puts his head against her belly.*) Let me hear!
Tell them it's me! Cohn! *Voices!* Name it! Cohn does it! No
more kidding around.

JOAN

(*Tries to break away.*)
I must go.

COHN

(*Holds her.*)
It's not fair!

(*They struggle.*)

JOAN

(*Begins to stagger.*)
You must let me—

COHN

Voices! (JOAN *topples over.* COHN *catches her in his arms.*)
What is this? (*To* ABE) What's the matter with her?

ABE

You did it again.

COHN

Joan. Don't joke, Joan. (*Drags her into the light.*) You want to
go? Is that it? Is that all you want? You're free. Free as a bird.
Go. Go, Joan. Go. (*Drags her to hole in the wall.*) You're free.
Did I say no? Wake up, Joan. Go. Go! Go! (*To* ABE) She won't
go.

ABE

She's dead.

COHN

She won't go. See? I'm holding her loose. What can I do? It's
her decision. Look how loose I'm holding her.

(JOAN *rises out of* COHN's *arms and floats high above his head.*)

JOAN

Farewell!

COHN

You'll hurt yourself!

JOAN

I am off.

COHN

Without me?!

JOAN

I'm off to heaven. Happiness is waiting. Fields of green, sunlight—

COHN

You can't get there that way! You need a rocket ship! You told
me so yourself!

JOAN

Not if you're dead.

COHN

You're not dead.

JOAN

I am dead.

COHN

No! I deny it!

ABE

Stop arguing! Can't you see she's dead?

COHN

If she's dead, why is she up there?

ABE

If she's alive, *how* did she get up there? Bow your head. A little respect.

COHN

(*Cannot bow his head.*)
How can I not see her for the last time?

JOAN

I am going far but I have come far. I have been several people, seen terrible things, had my heart broken and then spliced, have been shot at—

COHN

No!

JOAN

—have escaped, have been trapped, have escaped, have found God and lost him, found hope, lost it, grown weak, grown ill, passed out, recovered, walked on water, performed miracles, died, and floated up to the ceiling. And out of these myriad experiences I have learned all that I know and this is the sum of it: I have learned that however prosperous you should get out of the house, however satisfied you should be dissatisfied, however disillusioned you need hope, however hopeless you need patience, however impatient you need dignity, however dignified you need to relax, however relaxed you need rage, however enraged you need love, however loved you need a sense of proportion, however dispassionate you need passion, however possessive you need friends, however many friends you need privacy, however private you need to eat, however well fed you need books, however well read you need trials, however tried you need truth, and with truth goes trust and with trust goes certainty and with certainty goes calm and with calm goes cool and with cool goes collected but not so cool and collected you can't be hot and bothered. And if you're hot you need affection and if you're affectionate you want perfection, but however imperfect you needn't complain all the time. However lost you need to be found, however found you need to change, however changed you need simplicity, however simple not *too* simple or over-simple, however righteous not self-righteous; however conscious not self-conscious or self-hating or self-seeking; but you should be self-sufficient, but not alienated, not despairing, not sneering, not cynical, not clinical, not dead unless you are dead, and even then make the most of it. As I hope to do now. But first: My Last Will and Testament.

COHN

No!

JOAN

You must hear me.

COHN

It's not true!

ABE

(*To* COHN)
Now at the end a little respect.

JOAN

To Abe I bequeath my armor in the hope of inspiring strong resolve and the courage to find a conviction. To Cohn I bequeath my Voices because he needs all the help he can get.

FIRST VOICE

I won't go!

SECOND VOICE

I object!

(COHN, *in amazement, looks down at his stomach.*)

WISEMAN

(*Leaps up from his napping place and bangs gavel.*)
Objection overruled. Case dismissed.

(Scoops up JOAN's *armor and runs for the hole in the back wall.)*

ABE
(Starts after him.)
That's my armor!

WISEMAN
Miarma? That's in Florida!
(He leaps out of the hole, ABE *leaps after him. Both disappear from view. Sounds of a terrific struggle.)*

COHN
(Stumbles.)
Who's pushing me?

FIRST VOICE
Him.

SECOND VOICE
It's you I'm pushing, not Cohn.

COHN
(Stumbles.)
Well, quit pushing.

FIRST VOICE
Well, you tell him to quit pushing.

*(*COHN *stumbles backward.)*

COHN
Cut it out!

SECOND VOICE
You heard him.

FIRST VOICE
He meant you!

SECOND VOICE
You started it.

COHN

You didn't behave this way with Joan!

FIRST VOICE

We're influenced by our environment.

ABE

(*Rises into view, dressed in* JOAN's *armor, her sword raised in victory.*)
Onward!
(*Sword high, he stalks out of sight.*)

COHN

(*Runs to hole in wall.*)
Abe! It's pouring! You'll catch your death of cold! Viral pneumonia! A stroke!
(*Suddenly stumbles toward hole.*)

SECOND VOICE

Quit shoving!

(COHN, *struggling to stay erect, loses the struggle and tumbles backward through the hole, disappearing from view.*)

FIRST VOICE

Now you did it!

SECOND VOICE

Who did it?

FIRST VOICE

I didn't.

SECOND VOICE

No. You're the innocent one around here.

(COHN *rises into view, blinking in the strong sunlight.*)

COHN

It's not as bad as it looks. (*Holds out a hand.*) It's only a drizzle.   G 50

FIRST VOICE
It's getting better.

SECOND VOICE
By whose evidence?

FIRST VOICE
The evidence of my senses.

SECOND VOICE
Your senses should have their head examined.

COHN
Shut up. Follow me.

(COHN *walks off. Lights fade on* JOAN, *in space, apparently heaven-bound.*)

CURTAIN